Alcoholism
Taken Advantage of Drinking and Sober

JERSEY BILL

 www.trafford.com

North America & international
toll-free: 1 888 232 4444 (USA & Canada)
fax: 812 355 4082

This is a true story of my life, and my own opinions.

Dedication

To Carlos and alcoholics.

I'm also dedicating this book to alcoholics everywhere and to my brother-in-law, Carlos, who never had a drinking problem. He was a great husband and father that loved all people and also helped everyone. He died December 20, 2013, at the age of fifty-one years old. He was his mother's favorite child. She's ninety-two years old. The holidays are for family and friends, the season of giving, and this great man gave his life with a brain tumor. Three families are suffering today.

To my sister-in-law, a great man died, and also, to his sons, he'll never, ever, be replaced. It's hard.

Nobody expects death. Only Jesus knows. He wouldn't want anybody to beat themselves up. It's hard. I lost my father when I was thirteen years old. He is a powerful angel with Jesus now, and so is Carlos. His spirit is over all of us now and with love and happiness.

God bless you, Carlos. You will be missed by all you touched and in everybody's heart. Christmas will be never forgotten.

Thank you.

Love,
Jersey Bill and wife

Introduction

This is a true story of alcoholism. I feel that alcoholism travels through one generation to another. Children being abused, children being bullied, and even children being molested. My story starts with my father. He was born eighty to one hundred miles from Rome, Italy, and my mother, she was born in Muskegon, Michigan. This book consists of the truth and my own opinions of alcoholism and people who take advantage of people drinking and sober. You will be shocked with my saying "When doors begin to close, eyes begin to open." Don't let the doors close around you.

I hope I will help you.

God bless you.

Jersey Bill

Spigna Saturna, Italy—where my father was born

Spigna Saturna, Italy—where my father was born

My father was born April 19, 1931, in the mountains eighty to one hundred miles from Rome, Italy. My great-grandparents owned two villas in Italy. They were considered rich. These villas had farms, and they supported themselves that way. My father was the last child my grandmother had; she had six children—two boys and four girls. My aunt said it was beautiful there—mountains and flowers—but in those days, Italy was going with Germany, with Hitler. My grandmother was an American citizen. She went back to Italy when she was expecting my dad. So he was an American citizen born in Italy. They moved back to the United States when he was three years old. They left my aunt to take care of my great-grandparents. They were older at this time. The Germans were nasty; they would rape the young girls and kill them and the elders in the family. They had a room underground, a hiding place when the Germans were coming. Well, when the rest of the family came to the United States, they ended up in a Catholic home. There was the Depression still going on here, and my grandmother couldn't afford to feed them. My grandfather died when he was forty-five years old, mainly from drinking. He also had money. He owned two apartment buildings and a Tailoring shop with a shoe repair. When he died, my grandmother lost everything. The Depression hurt a lot of people in those days. My father was three years old when he came here. My dad loved his sister. My aunt, most of the time, was with him, watching over him.

My dad would be lost without her. One day the nun hit my dad, and Aunt told her, "You better never hit my little brother like that again." My dad was five years old at the time. My grandmother took kids out of the home when they were able to work, so she took my aunt out when she was fourteen years old, and my dad remained there. He was five years old; he cried when my aunt left. My aunt wasn't just a sister; she was like a mother to him. That was how much he loved her. When he was seven years old, he could speak Italian, Latin, and English. He was a smart little boy by now. He was the only one left in this Catholic home in New Jersey. I think other things happened to him in this home with the Catholic priest even back in the '30s. He also liked art; he could draw a person just sitting in front of him. Finally, in 1941, he was taken out of the home. He was eleven years old, and the family lived in the Bronx, New York. The Bronx in the '40s was a hard place to live; you had to fight to keep what was yours. My father would buy bags for half a penny and sell them for a penny to help feed his family. There was a black kid that picked on him all the time. My aunt Gloria would make my father fight him all the time even though the kid was bigger and older than he. My father had to work to help the family to eat. The older kids worked in a factory, but life was still hard. It was 1941; by now, my grandmother would go to the bar, pick up a man, bring him home, and while he slept, my father and Uncle Joe would rob him.

When my father was thirteen or fourteen years old, he stole a dress for his mother and did two years in a regular state home. That was where he learned to fight; he was good at that. He told my mom he had a lot of fights there. When he was fifteen or sixteen, he got out of the home and started to fight in Golden Gloves. He went looking for the black kid that bullied him and beat the hell out of him. The tables turned on the kid now. He also lied about his age and enlisted in the navy. They found him to be too young and discharged him, but the Italians wanted him to fight professionally, but my grandmother said no, and he listened to her. He was becoming a knockout puncher; he was really good.

He was a good street fighter too. He started working in an auto body shop; he was a very good body man. He was very strong by now.

My grandmother decided she wanted to move to Muskegon, Michigan. By now, my dad met a Mexican girl and loved her with all his heart. They had a baby boy. Before then, they, the Bronx's Italians, wanted my father to fight professionally. My grandmother said, "Now the people in the Bronx feared him." When he walked, the people would step to the side so as not to get in his way. One day, three girls beat up Aunt. My father went looking for them and told them, "If you don't plead guilty, her beatin' won't be nothing to the beating I give you three." They pleaded guilty.

Back to Muskegon, Michigan. My dad loved Gloria so much, but the family didn't like my father. They said he fought too much. He always had a hard life: the Catholic home then the wild streets of the Bronx, New York. He didn't let people take advantage of him. He always said, "I don't ask for respect. I demand it." My father and Gloria had a beautiful son, half-Mexican and half-Italian. Gloria was his first love. He was very strong too. He weighed 140 pounds and bench-pressed 250 pounds; he was like a little monkey. They called him Little Jersey.

He enlisted in the army with Gloria's brother in 1949. He knocked out his commanding officer and got a dishonorable discharge. His platoon went to Korea. They all got killed except him. Gloria's brother was killed too. My dad was really hurt by the death of Gloria's brother; they were good friends. Dad was a great auto body man with a lot of talent; he put his art in fixing cars.

Dad had a friend, Charlie; he was Italian too. His girlfriend was Donna, and she had a friend, Rae Jeanne, then Rae Jeanne started dating my father. She ended up being my mother. One day he brought Rae Jeanne to the T family. There was a bowl of salad on the table, and Rae Jeanne ate all the salad. Then in September 1950, they were married. My older brother was the first child born in the family. My dad worked at a body shop in Muskegon, a Buick dealership. It didn't take much to make my father angry. He was a good-looking man, strong, and could box; he also was a good street fighter.

One day they went to the movies. Mom was expecting my older brother. Some bigger man said, "Nice boobs." My father knocked out his teeth for the disrespect. He was raised in New York not to take anything from anybody; he always demanded respect. After my older brother was born in June 1951, he was twenty-one years old. He could drink in a bar, but Mom was still too young; she would sit at the tables, and he would sneak her beer. Wherever he went, a fight would follow. My mom wore glasses; her eyesight wasn't good, and a guy called her Goggle Eyes. Dad hit him then told him to say he was sorry; the man did.

His friend said, "You think you're a bad-ass?"

Dad said, "I know," and hit him too. The guy rolled down the hill. Dad just had that way about himself. He would fight on a drop of a dime when he drank liquor; with beer, it made him even more nuts. They moved around a lot. The police didn't like him always getting in fights and hurting men. His nickname was Little Jersey. That was his boxing name. He always made good money, and the family never went hungry. He enjoyed fighting people; that was his bad point.

They moved to New York. Mom didn't like it. That's where his sisters were. My aunt was married to my uncle Tony. They finally moved to California for their children's health. Everybody knew Little Jersey in New York, mainly in the Bronx, but Mom and Dad moved back to Muskegon, and he went back to work at the Buick dealership. The body men laughed at him when he had a little box of tools. They didn't laugh when he made twice the money they did; they were working on piecework. My father laughed.

Then in December 1954, my older sister was born. My parents were drinking more. At this time, Mom was old enough to go in a bar. They were fighting more. Between the two of them, Mom was a stay-at-home mother, and she would get bored taking care of two children. My grandmother was the first. My aunt was the second, and my older sister was the third generation of the same name. Dad was making great money, and he was partying and whoring around by now, and Mom was sitting at home. My mother's father, was a drinker too. He would bring beer for my mother and him; he loved Dad, but Dad was his own person. He did what he wanted. Then dad decided to open his own body shop; he didn't like working for other people. Everybody knew him in Muskegon; they knew he was a great auto body man. Even the black people came to him. Back then, in the early '50s, the black people would do hit-and-runs; they came by my father. He would work on their cars all night and charge them $350. That was a lot of money back then. He fixed a black man's car one time; the man owed him $450. He said he would pay him Friday. My father told him, "If you don't pay me, I will find you. If you're with your mother, father, wife, children, or with your friend, I will beat your black ass." Believe me, the man was there Friday. He found out his reputation as a fighter. He had a good business, but he couldn't stay in one place too long; he had to move to make more money all the time.

He always said hillbillies live in Muskegon, Michigan. They moved to New Jersey in 1957. Mom was expecting another child, then I was born November 1957. I had blond hair and hazel eyes; I was a cute child. My brother and sister had dark eyes and dark hair. In the beginning, he said, "Is this my child?" Mom said, "Yes, or none of the kids are yours." I was a sick child when I was born. My older brother was six years old, and my older sister was going on three years. My mom had us every three years almost. When I was ten months old, I had my to use the big-boy potties now. Mom would take me for a walk in my little red wagon, and people would give her money for me. I was a cute kid, and I would say, "Ice cream, Mommy." She took me for a sundae; I loved ice cream. I was the baby of the family, so I got away with a lot of things. Mom said my older sister and my older brother were jealous of me.

One day when I was four years old, Dad said to Mom, "I want to move to California." Now we were moving across the country, and Don's family moved with us. We looked like circus people: trucks pulling cars and a moving truck—even Grandpa moved with us. From the winters to sunshine all the time, Dad even bought another truck in Arizona—anything to make money. Dad found a road of dealerships. It was 1962. Now I was going on five years old. He had a compressor on his truck. He went from dealership to dealership fixing dents in cars. He made about $200 a day. There were about thirty dealerships there. On this long road, he was a hustler for money. We were living in a motel. I had another convulsion from a high fever. Dad put a spoon in my mouth so I wouldn't swallow my tongue and saved my life again.

Mom blamed him again, "You keep moving. You're going to kill my son."

He cried his eyes out again; he was starting to drink more. They were fighting a lot now. Mom had a marine on the side as a boyfriend, and Dad always had another woman. He found out about the marine, and he feared my father.

Dad told him, "I catch you on the streets, your ass is mine."

He stayed away. The Marine Corps didn't teach him enough to kick Little Jersey's ass.

I was in the hospital. I told my parents I wouldn't leave either. I had a sailor suit. He went crazy trying to find me a little sailor suit.

Alcoholism was hitting my parents hard. By now, Mom wanted to find a job; my father wanted her to stay home with the kids. My older brother was eleven years old, my older sister was eight years old, and I was five years old. Mom always wanted to go back to Muskegon, but Dad was making really good money now. He had another body shop. Don was working for him, and he got Grandpa a job delivering paint supplies to body shops. Grandpa was a beer drinker.

Dad told Grandpa, "No drinking on the job when you're working."

Grandpa made a couple delivers. He needed a beer and smashed up the delivery truck. Dad had to fix the truck for nothing and fixed the car he hit.

He was so angry with him. "Why, why did you do this?" He said, "I told you." But he forgave him; he loved Grandpa.

Grandpa would be in a bar. Mom would make Dad go get him. As soon as he saw my father pull in the parking lot, Grandpa would start a fight with the biggest guy in the bar, and Dad would have to fight this man because he wouldn't let anybody hit his father-in-law. Grandpa did that all the time.

Dad would say, "I'm going to kick your ass one day." But he never did. Grandpa was his buddy, but he would get angry with him.

We kids loved California. The weather was beautiful, but Mom always wanted to return to Muskegon, Michigan. Dad put it off as long as he could.

One day my older brother was saying bad words on the streets in California. A truck pulled over, and two men said, "You need your ass kicked."

My older brother said, "I'll tell my father."

They said, "Go ahead."

So my older brother went home.

My older brother said, "Dad, these two men want to hit me."

Dad went outside and said, "He's a little boy. He doesn't know better."

One guy said, "I'll kick your ass."

Dad said, "Let's go and play."

There was a parking lot at the end of the block. They started fighting. Dad knocked him out and broke his nose. On top of it, while he was knocked out, Dad told the other man, "You want to play too?" He picked up his friend and left. He knew better. These guys disrespected him and paid the price. He should have been a professional boxer like the Italians said in the '40s. He was just too good, and he knew it.

He went in a bar in California. The bar owner said something to him that he didn't like. He started tearing the barstools out of the floor (they were screwed on the floor) and started breaking the mirrors. He was in a blackout; he didn't remember that. He and Don stopped at the bar, and the guy said, "No more. I'll call the police. Get out of here."

Dad said, "What happened?"

He said, "You're nuts. No more."

It was a blackout. This started to happen more and more, so finally, we returned to Muskegon, Michigan. I was going on seven years old now. I was still six years old when we went back to Muskegon, Michigan. From beautiful weather to the cold, cold winters, Mom and Dad's alcoholism was getting worse. Mom drank like the fire department.

One day on, one day off—Dad was drinking and it continued almost every night, and we children had to watch it. The fights—they were bad. Dad opened another body shop and an Italian restaurant. He was running two businesses now. Mom was expecting again, another girl. Mom didn't want any more children; she had three kids already. After I turned seven, four months later, my younger sister was born.

My younger sister cried all the time. I was seven years old, my older sister was ten years old, and my older brother was thirteen years old. My older brother was buying books about the Marine Corps. Dad would get angry, I guess, because Mom had an affair with a marine. Dad had a minor heart attack. The doctor told him to give up one business, so he did the Italian restaurant, but he kept the body shop. He loved body work. My older sister took care of my younger sister, and Mom went back to work as a cashier in a food store. They both had affairs outside the marriage, Mom with the manager of the food store and Dad with a couple strange women, and life went on. We children, at that time, started to get abused, mainly my older sister and me. My younger sister was the new baby of the family. I guess I was jealous now.

Through these years, they would separate and get back together. Every time I had a high fever, Mom put Vicks on me, and Dad would make me drink hot wine and honey. I hated it. Then they would put me under blankets so the fever would break.

Don stayed in California, so Dad and Charlie would go out, then Don came back to Muskegon. He had other friends too, the Galey Boys. They started fights, and Dad would fight their battles; my father was sick of them. He was the arm-wrestling champ in the bars. A college football player came in one day. Charlie would have Dad arm-wrestle him. The guy was big, about six feet four inches; he had one hundred pounds on my father. They started; whoever won had to buy the bar a drink. Charlie had side bets. Dad locked his arm; the guy couldn't put him down. This went on for a long time. The guy released for a minute; Dad slammed his hand on the bar, and now the people couldn't believe it. Charlie now had a lot of money.

Charlie did this all the time.

Dad told him one more time. "Charlie, I'm going to kick your ass. I don't want to play these games."

He loved Charlie like a brother too. Charlie bought the Italian restaurant from him; one of his friends got involved too. They couldn't cook like Dad, so every now and then, Dad would prepare food for them, but he made them pay him. Charlie built a garage to do auto body work. He took in a job he couldn't fix. Dad would help him and charge him again.

He would tell Charlie all the time, "Don't take in anything you can't handle."

Charlie never listened; he always helped his friends. Don got laid off again. Dad fired two body men and gave Don a job.

He said, "They didn't know what they were doing."

The best one was when Charlie and Dad bought a boat. They put it on Lake Michigan. Charlie would come to the body shop to get the keys for the boat to go out on the lake. Dad was always busy in the body shop.

One day Dad said to Don, "Let's get a twelve-pack of beer and go on the lake."

Charlie wasn't coming around too much now. Well, Don and Dad went to the lake with a twelve-pack, and the boat wasn't there. Dad said somebody robbed the boat. Charlie had a key made, so he didn't have to drive to the body shop. The old man was pissed off the first time he wanted to use the boat, and Charlie was partying on it. Dad forgave him again. Charlie always did these things.

Don called Dad one day and said his remark broke down and asked Dad to fix it.

Dad came over and said, "The compressor was shot. You need another."

So they left the house for downtown Muskegon to get a used refrigerator for the food. They were driving three blocks away; the people were cleaning the house.

There was a stove and a refrigerator in the driveway. Dad said there was a guy who stole the refrigerator from them and put it in Don's home. Then Dad said, "Let's take the old one sell downtown Muskegon and see how long it takes to get a case of beer cold." Dad was angry. "You have a better refrigerator than me. What do the cleanup people do when they find the refrigerator gone?"

I was about eight-and-a-half years old. Dad came home and said we were moving to Florida—again, another move. My younger sister was a year in a half. My older sister was twelve years old. My older brother was going on fifteen years old. We came to find out Dad got another woman who was expecting a child. We already moved to Florida, and I had a half brother in Muskegon. We received a hospital bill. Mom was pissed.

She called Dad. "Bill? Why bill?

Dad denied it. The drinking in the house was every night now for him.

I learned how to swim at five years old. I loved swimming. We lived across the street from a YMCA. I would climb the fence to go swimming. The YMCA gave me a job: picking up towels. And I could swim for nothing. The towels were in the weight-lifting rooms. This bodybuilder would hit me in the head all the time. I told him I was going to tell my father; he didn't know him.

One day Dad went to the YMCA with me. "Why are you hitting my son?"

He said, "I'll hit you next."

Dad knocked him out right then, and there he told him, "You touch my son one more time, I'll kill you."

The bodybuilder would buy me potato chips and soda after that. All the time, I told him, "My dad will beat you up."

I had a friend. She was a girl. We always hung out. We would go by her grandfather's house. He would give us money for ice cream or candy.

One day I went there by myself; her grandfather tried to play with me. I was just a little boy, about nine years old. I ran out crying to home. Just like a woman who was raped, I blamed myself. My father had seen me crying.

He said, "What happened?"

I told him. He was angry. "Show me where he lives."

We got in the car and went over there.

Dad said, "Stay in the car. Whatever you hear, don't get out of the car." He went in the house and beat him too. He put him in the hospital.

I said, "Dad, why did he do this to me?"

All he said was, "He regrets it now."

That had a big effect on my life. I started to rebel at people. I felt dirty. I tried to forget, but the damage was done. My older sister and I would go roller-skating every Saturday. Dad figured I would forget this, but I couldn't. Dad decided to move to New Jersey now. That was where I was born, in 1957. It was 1969 now. I was about ten years old, my younger sister was three years old, Virginia was thirteen years old, and my older brother was sixteen years old. We were living in another motel.

One day we went by the place of Uncle Joe, Dad's oldest brother, for dinner in the Bronx, New York. Uncle Joe had three children: Paul, my wife, and Anthony. We had dinner, and all got sick from this Italian sausage except Dad; he didn't eat it. We were sick for a week; he took us to the doctor. Dad was doing work at a dealership on Route 46 in New Jersey, making extra money.

Mom was saying, "We have to get these kids back in school."

The car salesman said, "I have an apartment on Fourth Street, Passaic, sixty-five dollars a month."

That was the beginning of the end; we moved to Fourth Street, Passaic, New Jersey. Fourth Street, Passaic, New Jersey was the worst place we ever lived in, but Dad was making $800–$1,000 a week in

1967. That was a lot of money. I started to hang out with the bad kids. There I was, really rebelling now. Dad started to beat me more. I started smoking, sniffing glue and Carbona spot remover. I guess almost getting molested hurt me badly. Mom and Dad didn't send me for help. I also was getting bullied by the kids in Passaic. I had a friend named John; he was always in trouble. Dad and Mom were drinking real heavy now. I got caught stealing. Dad beat me again.

One day I went to Coney Island, New York, with Ray and Joe Sudol. They left me there. I asked the police for help; it was crazy. The people gave me money and bought me something to eat; the police took me to Manhattan then got in touch with Passaic police. They went and told my father. He met me on the bus.

There were riots going on about Martin Luther King's death, and Dad beat my ass the worst ever. "What the hell were you doing in New York?"

I said, "I'm sorry."

He wasn't showing any love to me or my older sister. He was too busy working, drinking, or whoring around. I think he started doing drugs too. My dad always said, "If you can't beat somebody, you beat them with something in your hands."

These two black kids started on me one day. I hit them with a baseball bat. I was put out of school. Dad went to school with me. There were the two black kids and their black fathers and a black principal. Dad said, "You're in trouble, son." I hit the kids in the legs with the bat. Dad said, "I would have hit them in the head if it was me."

One father said, "That Ginnie kid."

Dad told him, "I don't need a bat to beat your ass."

The other father knew Dad and how he could fight; he owned a bar. He told that father, "He would beat the hell out of you. Believe me, he's a hell of a fighter. If I were you, I would say I'm sorry."

He did.

My father had a rep in Passaic; they called him Knockout Jersey. The blacks were afraid of him. I was kicked out of school.

The principal said, "You're raising your kid the wrong way."

I had to go to a Catholic school next. My older brother quit school. And Dad told him, "Now you have to work. You're not sitting around and eating my food and doing nothing." Dad gave him a job with him in the body shop. My older brother was working his ass off now; he didn't like it. Dad was a hard-ass now. He would work every day and drink every night and come home drunk. Mom would drink at home. We were surrounded by it. Even my older brother started drinking. I was still hanging around Ray and Joe Sudol; they would steal all the time. I was smoking, sniffing glue and Carbona spot remover, getting high. I was caught stealing again.

Dad came, and he said, "What's wrong with you? Are you crazy?"

And I knew I was getting a beating again. I continued to rebel. On my twelfth birthday, I picked up my first drink and got drunk. My older brother's friend did that to me.

My older brother ran away from home—he was eighteen years old—and joined the Marine Corps. Our family was falling apart.

On Saturdays, Dad would buy beer. I stood next to him, and he would give me a little beer; he didn't know I was drinking already. He also would buy pizzas for everybody outside our apartment building. I was twelve years old, my younger sister was five years old, my older sister was fifteen years old, and my older brother was eighteen years old in the Marine Corps. My older sister and I went to Catholic school, then my older sister went to Passaic High School. I had a couple of older friends. Mom knew another friend's wife, a friend I would go visit all the time as they lived just a block away.

One day I went over. My friend wasn't home. I was watching TV with another friend. He tried to molest me; it was eight years old all over again. I ran out of his apartment. I went home and told Mom. She called my father, then she figured he was going to kill him. She called the Passaic police. Dad showed up with a tow truck and another body man. The police was taking my friend to jail. They said, "Jersey, we have him."

Dad told my friend, "You should kiss the ground these police officers walk on. If I got here first, I was going to beat your ass and chain you to that tow truck and drag you all over Passaic till you were dead."

It was on the street of downtown Passaic. I was deeply depressed. I really started to act like I hated myself. I was a twelve-year-old child living in a place where everybody picked on me. I wanted to leave Passaic, but Dad just showed me even less love. I looked up to him. I started to not trust adult men. I couldn't be alone with them now. It was two times. I had some friends that understood, but I had others that made fun of me; the hurt was really bad. They called me Bill and Another Friend on the Kitchen Table. When I was alone, I cried. I couldn't do my schoolwork right; I was a mess.

One night I fell asleep in my father's bed. He came home drunk and tried to molest me. I couldn't believe it—my own father, the man I looked up to all these years—me, his son. I wanted to die now the third time. I couldn't look at him. Here's a man who raised me, and this—I hated him. I told my mother what happened; she had him put in jail. She watched him in handcuffs. He cried.

"What's wrong? You play with your son, you son of a bitch. I hate you."

We didn't know this about our dad.

I felt hate toward him, but I also loved him. He was my dad. So many mixed feelings—I didn't tell anybody about this; I bottled it up. The judge told him he was lower than a snake, and he had to pay all the bills at home and give Mom a certain amount of money every week. He had to stay in a motel.

All his abuse was catching up to him. I started to run the streets and didn't care about anything. Dad would come by on Saturdays, give Mom money, and cry, "I'm sorry, Rae, please forgive me. Please." He cried to me, "Billy, forgive me, please, I love you so much."

After weeks of this, I still hated him, but I started to forgive him. He just wanted his family back.

He said, "I'll change." He was out for months. Now the court date came up. I looked at him. I just couldn't put him in jail for years; he was my father, no matter what. It was just the look on his face; even my mom felt bad. I told the judge it never happened, I made it up. I lied to the court. The judge and the detectives were mad at me; they wanted to lock him up and throw away the key. I had seen relief in his face. I just couldn't put him in jail. Mom let him come home. He was different; he tried to be a good father, but he wasn't trusted by us kids. I still went with him. I asked him if he loved me; he started to have tears come down from his eyes. I started to forgive him. I guess this situation, for us to be father and son—it was affecting him too. He liked to fight, and he started fighting a lot more now and drinking a lot. I'm not saying he was perfect. The Passaic police was after him all the time. They said he got away with trying to molest his child. They hated him. Dad's life was catching up with him.

He had a half-black, half-Italian friend; he was also like a brother to him. He told me, "Your dad could beat the hell out of anybody. He said if you disrespected him, he would just beat you up. He didn't talk. He'd punch your lights out—that's it." He told me stories about him. "Your dad, one day, was in Sugar Bills, a bar. He didn't like a man there. He was black anyway."

His friend, Randy, said, "Jersey, let it go. If you want to kick his ass, wait till we leave."

Dad said, "You're ready to go. I wanted this man bad."

Finally, Randy said, "Let's go."

Dad walked over and knocked the guy out. "OK, I'm done."

Randy said he did this all the time, just hit men. One day Randy said they went to Rutherford to drink. The bartender said, "No more, Jersey."

Dad said, "Just one more."

The bartender jumped up and said, "No more."

Dad knocked him out, went behind the bar, and poured another drink. He said, "I just wanted one more," like he had the rights to hit the bartender. He was locked up for that; he started to bend the bars on the jail cell. How strong do you have to be to do that?

Randy said, "Stop, Jersey."

The police let him go before he destroyed the jail cell and told him to stay out of Rutherford. This man told me these stories because on June 21, 1971, my father, John T., "Little Jersey," died. He was forty years old. It was Father's Day. I did love him. I was thirteen years old now, my younger sister was six years old, my older sister was sixteen years old, and my older brother was turning twenty years old in a week (he was stationed in Germany). Dad's mom came, Mom's mom came, Grandpa came, and Charlie, his friend, came too. Late, and the funeral was over. My older brother was there too. It was a sad day in our family. My father, dead at forty years old, was the youngest to die in the T family.

Before he died—it was three in the morning—he said, "Rae, I have to talk to you."

Mom said, "OK."

He said, "Rae, please forgive me for everything I did wrong." He told her everything that she didn't know. "I need your forgiveness."

She said, "I forgive you."

He said, "I'll be dead by nine in the morning."

Mom figured he had too much to drink. First he drank a sixty-four-ounce root beer and threw up. Mom said he never did that. He started to walk around the kitchen table holding his chest. He wouldn't let us out the door. He died at eight forty-five in the morning. Did he know, or did he kill himself for the life he lived? Nobody knows. He had a massive heart attack. The T family feels he killed himself. My mom said, "Your father lived two years for every year. He should have been eighty years old, but he was forty years old. He lived a fast life."

Where my parents were married in 1950

Docks in Michigan

Dad was a man that took nothing from anybody; he would help you if you were a friend. If you screwed him, he would beat your ass and never forget. Black bars, Spanish bars, Italian bars, or white bars showed him nothing but respect. He would hit first and ask questions later. He made mistakes—everybody does—but deep down, he loved my mother and his children. He wasn't well liked, but if he figured he was right, he stood his ground. I do blame his upbringing in the Catholic home—maybe a priest played with him—and his mother for not showing him the love he needed. He always said, "Keep your friends close, and keep your enemies closer." He said, "If somebody takes five dollars or five hundred dollars, kick their ass. They're trying to rob you." And he also said, "You make a person happy, you make ten people happy. You screw a person, you screw ten people. Word of mouth will hurt you. That's street logic."

Well, after the funeral, we moved by Grandma in Florida. My older sister loved a married black man. When my father was still alive, he beat her like a man over that, but he was dead now.

I miss Passaic. I don't know why so many bad things happened to me there, and Mom listened to us and moved back to Passaic. We stayed with people in Passaic, then we moved to the Projects Aspen Place. We were one of six token white families there. My older sister went with her black married boyfriend. Even Mom started dating black men. I went back to Catholic school in the eighth grade.

My younger sister was in the first grade, and I think Dad was turning in his grave. My older brother was back in Germany, on embassy duty in the Marine Corps. The family was going to hell fast. I was drinking and smoking weed now. I blamed my dad for our life now.

I ended up hanging out with the big guys behind Holy Rosary, the Catholic school I went to. I never stayed by the projects. I was ashamed of it. I had black friends when I went to high school, but I didn't trust them. I hung with the white guys, the Puerto Rican guys, the Polish guys, and the Italian guys; they all hung behind Holy Rosary Church. I started working in the high school, in a print shop; they had a program for kids there. I even bought my own clothes. I did that so there was more money for food to eat in our family. I guess I was a little like my father. I continued to drink and smoke weed, but I turned into a man. When Dad died, it wasn't easy. Life sucked—sometimes there were black men in our apartment, then my older sister was expecting from her black boyfriend. She was five months pregnant when my older brother came home from the Marine Corps. My older brother wanted to kill her and the black's baby. "Are you crazy?" He had locked himself in his room for two days before he came out. He blamed Mom and yelled at her. "You let this happen, Mom. Why did you come back here to Passaic, New Jersey?" He had gone out and gotten drunk for two days—so, so angry—before he came home again.

My older sister cried to him, "Please don't hate me. I'm sorry." My older sister respected my older brother and loved him a lot. My older brother wasn't ready to talk to her.

Weeks went by, and he said nothing to her. I didn't care. I was hanging with my friends and getting high. I think at the first drink at twelve years old, I became a child alcoholic. It took me out of the pain I felt from men trying to molest me; it made me into somebody else. I never wanted to be me. The little boy that loved ice cream replaced it with alcohol and drugs. Child abuse is a main factor to child alcoholism and drug addiction.

I had a friend, Danny. When we graduated high school, I was seventeen years old. I wanted to be a marine like my brother, so did Danny. We enlisted in the Marine Corps. When I went to boot camp in Parris Island, I decided I couldn't do this. I wanted out. Danny stayed in. He would be a great marine if his gun didn't backfire and blow the top of his fingers off. I came home first. See, I never wanted to be me. I wanted to be my older brother, then when I came home, I wanted to be a body man like my father. I didn't know what I wanted. I started to get drunk more and more. I was working in a body shop that Dad had worked at before he died, making eighty dollars a week, two dollars an hour, not caring about anybody but myself. My mom wasn't really showing me love; she was busy with my older sister and her daughter, Latonia, and my younger sister was hanging with her black friends. My older brother had a girlfriend; he moved in within a year. Before, I always loved my family, but I figured I was by myself. My older sister always caused problems with me, and my younger sister always acted like a little baby—Dad babied her till he died, and Mom continued to do the same. My father told me one time, "Your mother could be the biggest whore around, but she's your mother. Respect her and love her with all your heart." So I did, no matter what happened.

I continued to work. When I was nineteen years old, I asked my aunt if I could come to California. She said yes, so I went there. My mom didn't care, and my older sister loved the idea. I didn't see Aunt except at my uncle Joe's funeral about thirteen months before Dad died in 1970. He was forty-nine years old. I was twelve years old. A lot of things happened when I was twelve years old.

It was something when Uncle Joe died. Dad went for a walk with me. There was a little coffee house. The Italians talked to Dad in Italian, "I'm sorry to hear about your brother." Dad said, "Thank you." This was the first time I heard my father speak Italian. Dad decided he could get his card read to him. The lady said, "There will be another death in the T family in a year."

Aunt had a bad auto accident when she returned to California. Dad said no, not my aunt. Thirteen months later, it was Dad. One day, my aunt had a dream about Uncle Joe and Dad. They were on the street of the Bronx, New York. Dad and Uncle Joe were across the street. Aunt was crossing the street, and they said, "No, stay there." This was before Dad died. Aunt said Jesus was telling her something. She loved her brothers a lot, and she lost both of them in thirteen months' time. Life tells you things. Sometimes you just have to watch.

When I got to California, my uncle had a job for me. He was a city worker, and he was a supervisor there. I became a tree trimmer with my boss, Jay. It was a beautiful January, and it was in the '70s. New Jersey had snow and cold weather. I still missed my mother, but I was working. My cousin, my ex-wife, lived behind us, and her husband worked for the city too. She had two sons, Larry Jr. and Steven. They were good kids. I liked them. I would take the kids to play pinball around the block. I would give them five dollars in quarters, and I would sit and have coffee. So I was working for the city of Lawndale, California. This was in 1976–1977. I didn't have a beer or some weed for at least two months. I wanted a beer so bad.

There was a guy working there who asked me if I wanted to come over to have a couple beers. One day after work, I said, "Damn right." I came home high. Aunt and Uncle Tony were Christians, so they were at church. My aunt's son, Gary, was a Christian pastor. I did believe in Jesus, but I wanted to party too.

One day I took a walk. I talked to a guy who owned a body shop, and he offered me a job, part-time, three nights a week. I guess I missed body work too. I don't know why I started to miss Passaic, New Jersey again. I had no friends in California. All I did was work and go to church; it wasn't my cup of tea always praying. Well, this went on for about five months, and I wanted to go back to Passaic, New Jersey. Even when an alcoholic changes a place, he still brings the alcoholic with him. I was back in Passaic, and then I missed California. I was so screwed up going to California and coming back to Passaic, New Jersey. I didn't know what I wanted. I was still drinking and still smoking weed, but not too much, just now and then. I guess I still loved my mom too much. My older sister always caused me problems with my mom. My friends were still partying behind Holy Rosary, and we were also hanging out in Bill;s Happy Hour, a bar. I still had my friend John, but he was only for himself. I had a friend, Tom Jendrey. On Sundays I went there with a six-pack of beer. He always had Southern Comfort and some weed. I was always able to work, but I liked being high. At this time in my life, I was about twenty years, still lost and drinking. I was worse than my father at twenty years old. I noticed my friends. They worked in Passaic, drank in Passaic, and lived in Passaic, not going anywhere, so I decided to go back to California.

I tried the Christian religion this time. I didn't know about AA, so I went to church, plus I wouldn't admit I was an alcoholic at twenty years old. I worked every day. My mom always told me alcoholics drink wine and wash widows in the

Bowfly in New York. That wasn't me. Little did I know. I was living with my cousin Gary, the Christian pastor, so I had to sneak drinks.

My older brother's girlfriend got in trouble when they were living in South Gate, Michigan, so I had a lawsuit. I won. He asked me for help; he wanted to come to California. Cathy got caught stealing and was getting jail time. I had to help my brother. Aunt told me I was making a big mistake. I didn't listen.

We rented a little house in Costa Mesa, California. Dad's friend Don lived there. I got a job in a body shop. They drank. I drank. I was at home. My older brother also liked to drink. Remember, generation to another generation. If I didn't party after work, I partied at home.

I turned twenty-one years old. They had a big party for me. I was legal in California now. Alcohol and weed were all over the place. I was sitting in a bar. I heard a voice. I said, "I know that person." It was my friend Richie from Passaic, New Jersey. He also left Passaic for a better life, and we partied my birthday away. We started to hang out, but he was a sick ass, and I guess I was too. We went to concerts together, drank, and smoke weed. One day we went to the battle of the bands at UCLA campus. I had seen two parents and two kids with tuxedos on and green hair. I was stoned from weed. I started to laugh so hard. They also had sneakers on.

Richie said, "Shut up. We'll get killed here."

I couldn't; it was just so funny. I had never seen that before.

My older brother and I lived together about three months, then I think they didn't want me around after I saved Cathy's ass from going to jail. Aunt was right. I didn't have much money left. I did buy a car. I was used by my family. I was hurt over this. I told Don.

He said, "Billy, what goes around comes around."

I didn't know what to do. When I wasn't working, I was drunk. I felt lost. I went to a party the cook a pig underground a lava roast they call if I was drinking and smoking weed. I was drunk and stoned. I ate and continued feeling sorry for myself, so I decided to go by Richie's. On the way there, I hit a light pole at about twenty miles per hour. My teeth, about two of them, shot through my lip. I was bleeding, and I totaled my car. I took off to Richie's house. The police were looking for me. I had to get rid of the car. I called my older brother; he sent a tow truck to pick it up. There was a Marine Corps officer across the street; he looked at me. I said, "Please don't say anything."

He said, "You need help."

I said, "I know."

I moved across the street from my cousin Gary back in Culver City, California, and an old lady owned the house. I got another job in a body shop. Things were going good, and my alcoholic ways. They had a bar there, Whiskey Joe's. I stopped and had a beer or two, but before I knew it, I was getting drunk again after work, hanging out with drinking people. This old lady had a daughter married to a police officer from Culver City; he didn't like me, or he didn't trust me. I was taught respect for my elders. I just liked to drink.

One day these two black guys took me to a go-go bar in Los Angeles. I was having a good time partying, watching the girls shake their asses. It was great.

I didn't figure they were setting me up. I ended up sleeping on a floor in somebody's house. I didn't know. I realized I was robbed when I noticed all my money was gone. The house was on a main street, two blocks from where I lived. The old lady called the police there. The husband of the old lady's daughter wanted to lock me up. The old lady said, "No, he just went to sleep. Nothing else." I thank God for her. He had it out for me; he went to the home. I was renting a room, and he had me put out. I was homeless.

I was almost twenty-two years old now. I ran into a Marine Corps recruiter. I explained I was in the Marine Corps when I was seventeen years old, and I got out because I couldn't take it. I told him I had no place to live. I told him I was losing it.

He said, "You ever think about going back in the Marine Corps?"

I figured they wouldn't take me. It would be a way to prove myself to my family, my friends, and myself. I felt bad I didn't become a marine, so I decided yes. My life was going nowhere, so I started to train, running, working out, still drinking, but not as much. I was sleeping with my girlfriend, training, and working side jobs for money. When I was twenty-two years old, I went in front of a Marine Corps officer and asked him to give me another chance to be a good marine. He okayed me back in the Marine Corps. I told him, "You won't be sorry." I was ready. I went to MCRA, California. I already knew what they did to men coming in; it was hard, but I knew I could do it. I wasn't seventeen years old anymore. They shaved my head again. I was put in a platoon. The drill instructors knew I was coming back in my Marine Corps. Again they put me in physical training. I took it like a man.

Whatever they did, I was ready for them. I even said, "You won't break me this time." Then they started to lay off me. I was doing pretty good. I was being a marine. It didn't hurt no more. We went to the rifle range to learn about the M16 rifle. We were in a classroom, at the bleachers.

The drill instructor said, "Fall into formation."

I jumped off the side of the bleachers. My ankle and knee buckled. I wanted to cry; I couldn't get up. All I said was, "I fell again." I ended up in MRP, a medical platoon, for a month. Then they put me in another platoon. The leg was too painful, so I was discharged again. First time, I didn't want it; second time, I wanted it, but my body didn't want it.

I went back to Passaic, New Jersey. Like a hurt pup, I started working with a friend again at a body shop trying to forget everything. I started drinking heavily, then living in a rooming house. I worked and felt drained, feeling sorry for myself. A year later, 1981, I went to a doctor. He said I had a tear in my knee. It was a military injury. I had the surgery, and he put in a claim with the VA. They denied everything even after I was in MRP, the medical platoon; they were lying. Then the doctor called the VA lying bastards. I never expected they would screw me. I didn't have the accident on purpose; it just happened. I was twenty-three years old now. I figured I had no rights, so I just continued to work. The doctor told me I was going to have a lot of problems with my knees later in life. I started to work spraying office furniture and working at the body shop part-time, making good money working and drinking.

Drinking followed me everywhere. I was going to the go-go bars with my boss, Tommy, from River Drive Collision after spraying office furniture on my second shift, drinking after work. We always had a cooler of beer in the truck. Life was OK. I did this for about a year. When I had a problem with a painter at the office painting job, he tried to fight this black guy, and he got his ass kicked. He wanted me to lie. I said, "No, that was your fault, not the black guy's fault." He got me fired. I went to work at River Drive Collision full-time now. I didn't care. I drank, but I wouldn't lie for anybody. I always had a job no matter what. I was taught to work at a young age, so I did. I was living in a rooming house drinking and working, not going anywhere. The landlady said I needed a woman in my life. I was seeing women; I just liked being single, being able to come and go as I pleased. Now my older brother was getting in trouble in California. His drinking was affecting him with the law, just like Dad. My younger sister was graduating high school. My little sister and my older sister and Latonia were living with Mom. My older sister had another married black boyfriend; he was a nice guy, Wilbert. So I met an Italian girl, my ex-wife, one Sunday with my landlady. She was OK. But I didn't know I was good-looking, with blond hair and hazel eyes. She was all right. Well, we started dating. I was twenty-four years old, and I said to myself, "Maybe a good woman could change me." Her mouth would get on my nerves; she would start in all the time. We broke up and went back. This continued. I started messing with a real pretty black girl and a Colombian girl. I was still messing around with my ex-wife too. I knew my ex-wife's mother, father, brothers, and sister. My ex-wife was like her father, a big mouth.

I don't know what was on my mind. I asked my ex-wife to marry me; she said yes. My father always said Italian women are diamond earrings—they want to control everything. He was right. We would break up and go back engaged. It was a crazy relationship, but I continued with her, for I figured she would change. I had my own apartment in Passaic. I still had other women coming over. My ex-wife went home at night. My Columbian girl worked in a liquor store, and she would bring over something to drink and spend the evening with me.

Then the black girl came over for sex; it was great. I felt like a player, but in the end, I married my ex-wife. What a big mistake. I was twenty-six years old.

We got married July 14, 1984. It continued— her mouth and my drinking. We would just argue all the time. My older brother was back in New Jersey. Now at my wedding, he introduced me to cocaine, so every now and then, I did some cocaine with drinking. I was working at a body shop in Ridgewood, New Jersey. Now it was closer to home. I was a painter there, still having problems with my ex-wife. My younger sister had her own apartment now.

One day I ended up in a hospital. I said I wanted to kill myself. I was drunk. They figured I was serious. They put me in Greystone. The doors locked behind you. It was a nuthouse—such crazy people there. One day a girl had sex with two guys at one time. I said, "What the hell am I doing here?" I talked to a counselor, and after a week, I was released.

I went home to my ex-wife again. I still didn't think I had a problem drinking. I just said I had to watch what I say. I had a beautiful Pontiac Catalina, so real pretty. I took my ex-wife's car to the mechanic, and she used my car to go to work. She was hit by an armored truck and totaled my beautiful Catalina. I blamed her for that.

It was never right. After that, I had Tommy from River Drive Collision fix it. I lived in Prospect Park, New Jersey. I went to Passaic one day on a Sunday.

My friend Jorge and I were drinking and doing cocaine all day. I was driving home. I was out of it; the police pulled me over, and I got a DWI. This police officer came down, brought me a cup of coffee as soon as I sobered up a little, and gave me some cigarettes and asked me if I ever heard of AR I said, "Yes, the winos that wash windows."

He said, "No, I'm a recovering alcoholic, and I want to help you."

A police officer was an alcoholic—I couldn't believe it. I couldn't drive for six months at court in Elmwood Park, New Jersey. I started to go to AA meetings with the police officer from Elmwood Park. His name was Pete. I was OK, but I still didn't think I had a problem. These people lost homes, women lost children, and some lost their marriages. I even heard a guy who killed somebody in a blackout. I was comparing, not identifying. It was a matter of time, and I started drinking again.

One day my ex-wife and I were arguing. She called the police. I had to leave. I went by my younger sister's. I took my chances and drove there. I wasn't working in Ridgewood no more. I was working at Van's Auto Body in Haven, New Jersey. I had to take a bus to work every day. I did it for a while, then I found a job closer to Passaic. I always ended up back in Passaic. For six months, I would ride the buses. I worked at David's Auto Body, and I would work at Laplaca's Auto Body too. They were in Garfield, New Jersey. I caught the 209 bus to work, and it dropped me off at the bar Dutties Pub every night.

My younger sister and I went to Trenton after six months, and I had my license restored. It was expensive. I paid a fine and a $1,000-a-year surcharge for three years. My sister broke up with her Columbian boyfriend and started dating a black guy, Nathan. I tried to go back to the Columbian girl, but she said no, she had a boyfriend. My ex-wife took me to court for wife support, twenty dollars a week. I said, "What a mess my life is," but I continued. I worked for a guy that loved cocaine at Laplaca's Auto Body. I had a friend, Michele. She was married. She and I would have sex every now and then. My ex-wife filed for divorce, and we were divorced. It wasn't that I didn't love her; we just couldn't get along. I found a job at Tri-Boro Auto Body in Fair Lawn. Every Thursday we worked late till 9:00 p.m. I was twenty-nine years old now. Then we would drink beer, my kind of place. I would go to Benny's Luncheon for coffee every morning. I met a waitress the my ex-wife. She seemed nice. She had a nice ass. I told her one day we had to go out to dinner. About a week later, she invited me over for dinner. We joked around. She seemed sweet. The first dinner, we had sex that night. I was in love.

I worked Tuesdays and Thursdays late; she would bring me dinner on Tuesdays. I think the other body men were jealous. On my birthday, she sent a belly dancer. Everybody celebrated my birthday at Tri-Buro Auto Body.

I had an apartment in Paterson now. I asked her, "Would you like me to move in?"

She said, "Yes. I had a roommate." So he took over my apartment. She wanted to get married. This was the sick alcoholic mind. I was divorced September 21, 1987, and I remarried December 21, 1987.

She was three months expecting. I had all these bills to pay. I had to work.

My older brother said, "I'm sorry, you learn by your mistakes."

Finally, my daughter was born. My daughter had blond hair and hazel eyes like her dad. I was so proud that I had seen this beautiful little girl. She melted my heart my mom put it in the my wife Jersey and ex-wife had a little girl named my daughter it was in the my wife. I came to find out my ex-wife worked at the my wife. She started calling and saying we had sex last night, and it was really good. My ex-wife started yelling at me. I was still working two jobs. I told her, "She's doing this to cause problems between us. She's jealous of your two jobs everyday." And a fight every night. I finally called the my wife and told them my ex-wife was fired. I didn't hear anything from her after that. My ex-wife was still starting in now. I figured Tri-Buro Auto Body was right. I started to drink again really heavy. My ex-wife left me with my daughter. I was really feeling sorry for myself drinking, then I ended up in detox in a hospital in Passaic. I didn't do it for myself. I did it to get my wife and daughter back. I kept trying to call her. See, in detox, you can't use the phone. I got caught and was kicked out of detox. I already lost the apartment. I went back to work, but my head wasn't at the job. I was drinking and crying in my beer. It just continued.

I went to another detox at the hospital. Martin's Auto Body held my job. After two days, I went in a rehab for twenty-eight days. I was allowed to leave to go to work; they made me a lunch every day. I was saving money again.

I would see my daughter on Saturdays. I was working on myself. The twenty-eight days was up, then my ex-wife would start in again. I think she didn't want me sober; she couldn't control me. So like a good alcoholic, I started drinking again, then we would get back together again. As soon as I paid the rent, she would want me out. This kept going on. I figured she was Satan's daughter.

One day she said, "Your dad and I would get along."

I told her, "My dad would have beat your ass. You're mistreating his son." I could never hit a woman. If she were a man, I would have really beaten her ass. It was like a forty-forty. One day she would be good, the next day, a pain in my ass. I couldn't help drinking. I was losing jobs everywhere. I kept staying for my daughter now and coming back.

I got a good job in Upper Saddle River, at Ramsey Auto Body, making sixteen dollars an hour. I liked it with some good guys—no drinking. It was beautiful. I would bring bagels every day. They had a secretary working there, a nice person. My ex-wife accused me of sleeping with her; she was just sick in the head. I just went to work, and sometimes, I was sorry to go home at night never knowing what would happen again at home. I got her ex-husband a job with me cleaning cars. At lunch time, he would drink; he was worse than me.

I told him, "Another friend, if Jimmy catches you, he'll fire you."

He never listened. My personal problems caused me to lose my job. I said to my ex-wife, "You have to stop." She started calling the police, and I got locked up. I was released the next morning. I picked up my car and went by my mother. I filed for unemployment, and I wondered what I would do next. People figured I was nuts—I kept going back for more.

Many times in between, I tried to get sober; it just didn't work, so like an ass, I tried again with my ex-wife. Another apartment in Garfield—that was our third apartment in Garfield, New Jersey. I got a good job working in Totowa, New Jersey on Union Avenue as a painter. I gave her $400 a week for the house, went to work every day, and didn't drink much. Friday was payday. I would buy Italian food and a six-pack for me.

One day when I was crossing the street, my ex-wife pulled over. See, every time my ex-wife would break up with somebody, she wanted me back. She had a daughter by a married man, and her last name was T. I told her, "That's not my child. Why didn't you name it after the father?"

She said, "My name is T."

But that was just because of marriage. I told her to leave me alone. My ex-wife was never satisfied; the more you gave, the more she wanted. She was using my daughter as a weapon against me like a loaded gun. She knew I loved that kid. Her other daughter, Tracy, moved in; it was two against one. Every time I would pay the rent, she wanted me out. She went back to work when my daughter was a year and a half. I was trying to hold it together. I think she started to mess around with other guys she met as a waitress. She went back to work at Benny's Luncheon. I even started drinking with her ex-husband, another friend. I lost another job.

One day another friend and I were drinking at Terry's Bar. My ex-wife called the Elmwood Park Police, and I got my second DWT in the same city as the first one. I couldn't believe it. After that, my ex-wife and I separated for good. She started to use my daughter like she never did before.

One time I was in another rehab turning point. My ex-wife sent me a letter. I showed it to the counselor I had, and he said, "She's an alcoholic without a drink." She acted like an alcoholic without a drink, the same ways she accused me of having sex with everybody. I kept saying she was Satan's daughter. With one ex-wife to another ex-wife, it was like jumping from the frying pan in the fire. I was giving eighty to a hundred dollars a week; she took me to court to get more. I was making nine dollars an hour on the books. The court gave her forty dollars a week; she lost. She was mad. I figured I had seen smoke come out of her head. She told me I would never see my daughter again. That was her Italian ways. My little sister was a fighter like her dad.

She said, "If I catch her, I'm going to kick her ass."

My younger sister had a child by a black guy. My older sister was living with a guy from Haiti. Now even Latonia was a mother with a little girl. My older brother finally admitted he was a father; he had a little girl before he went in the Marine Corps. She was expecting back in 1969. My older brother's daughter married a Mexican guy named Marty; he was in the army. He was a grandfather at thirty-eight years old. This family changed so much since Dad died.

I was drinking so much over my daughter. I would go to a detox when I started to get sick. I would attend AA meetings but never take them seriously. I had an accident on the job with my knee. I always had problems since the Marine Corps; it just worsened. The Marine Corps never wanted to admit to the damage they did to me. My life was in a mess again. I blamed Jesus for my problems. I wasn't seeing my daughter, paying child support, not thinking my drinking was causing my problems. It was my family, my wife, but not me.

One thing I did right was, I would stop maybe eight weeks and drink for a week. I ended up in a detox rented room losing them and losing jobs. Then

I started to have knee surgeries on my left knee, one after another. I finally divorced my ex-wife October 10, 1994 (our first date was October 10, 1987, seven years to the date). I was hitting all kinds of bottoms and didn't see them. I would go to AA meetings and do it my way, not AA's way. I couldn't accept alcohol was kicking my ass. I wouldn't talk about my past except my daughter. When it came to my childhood, I would shut down about men trying to molest me. I was ashamed of that. I ended up on SSD at forty years old because of my left knee.

My mom was trying to be a mother now. All those years she treated me badly because of my older sister; she also wished death on me. My ex-wife moved my daughter to Pennsylvania. By now, I didn't see my daughter for three years. Traveler's insurance from my injury was always trying to screw me with money too; insurance companies are good when you're paying, but when you get hurt, they want to screw you. I was suffering since 1993 with this accident and had many surgeries. I took to the bottle really bad. Believe me, I wanted to die. I figured I would drink myself to death. The women I married screwed me, I wasn't seeing my daughter, I ended up in every detox in the state of New Jersey, and I still didn't think I had a problem. Going to AA and not listening, the people said I had a death wish. By now, my older brother and Cathy broke up; he was going nuts. They were together nineteen years. My older sister was with her boyfriend from Hatti, Latonia still lived with my older sister and her daughter, and my younger sister was living with Mom (she had a boyfriend; he was black, and he was a good man). I think Mom cared about him because he was like Dad. He didn't take anything from nobody, but he couldn't fight like Dad.

In February 2000, I had a total knee replacement on the left knee. I never felt so much pain in my life. I was sober at the time, going to AA. It was finally sinking in a little bit. I picked up for the last time. I was drinking and taking hydrocodone, which would kill anyone, but an alcoholic isn't afraid of anything. I had money in the bank. I was renting a room on Naw Avenue, Passaic. I let a person from AA stay with me.

One day I was in St. Mary's Hospital in Passaic. I was sick. I told my lawyer I wanted to die. He sent the police. That was how I ended up in the hospital. I left the hospital and rented a motel room and started drinking again. I was really trying to kill myself. Maybe I was a little afraid, so I called my sponsor. He sent a couple guys from AA. They didn't say much; they even took me to get more alcohol and drink a case of beer and a bottle of vodka. They were getting me so drunk I couldn't fight with them anymore. I was in sad shape. I drank all the way to the detox. This was my final bottom. Like I said, I hit a lot of bottoms, but this time, something sunk in.

I signed myself out of the detox and rented a motel room in Little Ferry, New Jersey. I said, "Jesus, please take the drinking or take me to you." Know that all the years I drank, two women told me my father's spirit was over me. Sometimes I would look up. I started to take AA more seriously. I guess Jesus helped me. I started to do it AA's way, not mine. People were being. I could pick up a drink again, but I didn't. I had an old man named Al.

He even said, "Billy's drinking is over."

I was working the program. I did know how to get drunk. I had to be teachable to be sober. I was forty-two years old. I also said, "Dad, I have you by two years."

I went to meetings every day and stayed sober. If anything, I didn't pick up a drink. Life started to get better. I had my own apartment in Garfield, New Jersey. I celebrated ninety days. I was still a little crazy. My sponsor said, "Keep coming." I had hydrocodone for pain. They told me to throw it away. I didn't want to, but I did. I went to my first New Year's Eve party with AA, a sober dance holidays. I surrounded myself with AA people. In the end of my drinking, I was sober for eight weeks, then I would pick up every eight weeks. I went through hell. Sobriety is good; you have to take one day at a time.

I finally surrendered to alcohol. It wasn't easy. Every time I had self-pity or anger, I turned to a drink. When I was sober four to five months, my brother tried to get me to drink because the focus was on him and he didn't like it. For years, I tried to stop, and I couldn't.

One day I had a bad cold. I met Mom for breakfast. I was sick. My eyes were red, and so was my face. The first thing she said was, "You've been drinking." I couldn't blame her because she had seen me look like that drinking.

I said, "No, Mom, I have a bad cold." See, you make family just as sick as you are. There were a lot of things I had bottled up for years. I had to get rid of my childhood that was hard and the two marriages I had. I didn't trust women too much, so I just worked on myself. I would see women but just as friends. My sponsor told me no relationships for a year and a half. Not drinking, everything started to work again. I said no sex.

He said, "You can have sex. You just can't get involved."

That was hard for me, but I had to listen.

He told me, "You have to learn to love yourself before you can love somebody else."

Then before you know it, I celebrated a year of sobriety. I was so proud of myself—a year sober.

I went to meetings where people celebrated years of being sober. I asked how.

They said, "One day at a time. Just keep coming."

So I did. My family didn't believe it. I finally took my ex-wife to court about my daughter. It was seven years since I had seen her. I told the judge this, and I told him my child was in Pennsylvania. He said that it was against the law to move the child out of state without my consent; the child support was stopped. My ex-wife called my lawyer and said she wanted her child support. My lawyer told her it was stopped because of lack of visitation. She was mad.

The Passaic County Probation made me go to court again. Another judge stopped the child support. After that, the Passaic Country Probation never bothered me again. It pays to be sober. My ex-wife asked my lawyer to change my daughter's last name.

I said, "No, I'll have my cake and eat it. No support and no name change."

She was pissed off.

Once I became sober, I went after everybody. Next was the UA. I ran into Tom Jewdrey when I first got sober. See, alcoholics either die or find AA. Tom had been sober for seventeen years. We started going to meetings together. We drank together. Now we were sober together. Life was great.

When I was sober for a year and a half, my sponsor told me to get my driving license back. I didn't drive for ten years now. He told me it was time. The money I owed was $4,500. I started to pay it all. This time I would ride a bus. I had seen this girl; she got off when I got off. I always said, "Nice ass." I was driving. I picked her and her girlfriend up by the bus stop. In the beginning, she didn't want to go, but there were two of them and one of me. It was cold. It was in the winter, so they got in the car. I would drive them to work and say, "Have a nice day." I did this every morning.

After a week, I asked her if she liked to go to dinner. I came to find out she couldn't speak English; she was Columbian.

It was hard talking to her. The first dinner was at an Italian restaurant. I couldn't speak Spanish, and she couldn't speak English, so the Italian waitress talked to her in Italian, and she understood some of it. She ordered dinner. (Funny, isn't it? I didn't know Italian was so close to the Spanish language. No wonder my father understood Spanish too.) I didn't know if a relationship would start. We couldn't talk to each other. She was a beautiful woman inside and outside. She even wanted to go with me to AA meetings. She had been married two times. And being burned, you just don't trust women too much—you think they're all alike.

I took her to an AA New Year's Eve party. We danced and had dinner, and at midnight, we held each other. She was with me all the time. She even had some clothes in my apartment.

In the morning, I would take her to work, buy her coffee and a butter roll, and give her lunch money then pick her up at night from work. This went on for about six months.

Then we moved in together. My two wives can't clean her doorstep. She loves me. In August 2003, we moved to North Carolina.

We were married on my father's birthday, April 19, 2004. We bought a home in Henderson, North Carolina. This April was our tenth anniversary, and we've been together for over twelve years now. See, I had two wives, but they didn't love me. My wife loves me, and I can never replace her. She was sent by Jesus. I'm not saying life isn't perfect, but it's a lot better being sober. My best day drunk isn't better than my worst day sober. I made a saying, "When doors begin to close, eyes begin to open." All my doors close on me, then my eyes open up.

I'm celebrating on April 25, 2014, fourteen years of sobriety. I never had almost fourteen years sober. I started at twelve years old. I even bought a new truck after eleven years of sobriety, a 2012 Ford Explorer XLT.

If I had kept drinking, I would be dead today. Jesus and AA saved my life. My father was dead forty-one years, and I had a spiritual awakening with him. I heard of people having them, but I didn't believe it would happen to me. He said, "I'm proud of you. I love you with all my heart. Stop helping family and friends. Fight for what you believe, and when you die, my hand will pull you up."

I cried like I was a thirteen-year-old again. Just because you stop drinking, you have to deal with a problem—that's life. But now you have the tools to deal with it. If you feel like drinking, call somebody in AA, or go to a meeting. The saying is one alcoholic helping another alcoholic. I'll say something to the newcomer: Take two dollars a day, and put it to the side. After ninety days, you'll have $180. If your life isn't somewhat better, go refund all your pain. Liquor stores don't close, and bars are still open. There's always an ass to take your place.

God bless you all. Give AA a chance, and find a Higher Power.

Jersey Bill

My first story is about the service. I won't mention the branch or anything else. I want it to say my first story.

I enlisted in the service when I was of age. I ended up getting hurt. I wanted to be a soldier, but my knee and ankle gave on me. I ended up in a medical platoon. My knee and ankle couldn't handle it. A year later, I had my first knee surgery. My doctor put in a claim, but they denied it. The doctor said I was being screwed; the medical platoon proved I was hurt. I started having problems with my knees and ankles. I started to drink a little more after this. I was falling apart little by little in the '90s. My knees really started to give me problems about 1993. I started to celebrate surgeries like birthdays every year. In 1997, I was on SSD. I was forty years old. You start to live at forty. I started to die. My drinking by now was really bad. Even in 1993, I was watching myself go to hell, and in 2000, I had a total left knee replacement. I was forty-two years old. This happens to people in their seventies and eighties. The service said I had a claim. What happened to the over twenty years of no claim? How many men and women had this happened too? I also became sober in 2000.

Today I'm fighting for what's owed to me, and they're giving me a hard time. Anything I ask for, they deny. It's like getting hurt again. When you enlist in the service, you're promised the world, but if something happens to you, then they kick you to the curb. I've been sober for fourteen years now, April 25. I do believe Jesus and AA saved my life. I have a beautiful wife today, and I'll never stop fighting for what I believe. See, in sobriety, you have to deal with life on life's terms. Most alcoholics turn to a bottle. Today, I turn to Jesus and AA.

God bless you all.

Jersey Bill

My book, *Alcoholism Taken Advantage of Drinking and Sober*, second story.

Moving to North Carolina

I had over three years of sobriety when I moved here. I always wanted to buy a home after I married my wife. I ran into a man who said he was a builder and had a real estate license. I gave him $15,800. See, when you're sober, you have to learn to trust people. It was one of the biggest mistakes I ever made; he was lying about everything. I did find a home, but with a lady that did have a real estate license. I had to take the man to court to get my money back. I sued him in civil court for three times the money and won in 2005, plus 8 percent interest. It came to $47,400. He hasn't paid a dime. It's at least $150,000 now, with interest. See, in sobriety, you have to deal with life on life's terms. If I were drinking, I would have tried to do a lot of damage to him, but being sober gave me a chance to change. If you don't change, you'll drink again.

God bless you.

Jersey Bill

Alcoholism Taken Advantage of Drinking and Sober, third story.

About the Love for My Mother

I was told by my father to respect and love my mother with all my heart. I was sober, going on eight years in December 2007. My mother had mercer. She said she was dying. I left North Carolina for New Jersey right away. I rented a motel room in Secaucus, New Jersey. While I was taking a shower, the ceiling fell in on me. I felt like I was dying. They called for the police and medical treatment. I felt they didn't want to be bothered, so I waited till I got home a day later. I had six months of back and neck adjustments, plus a scraping of the bone on my right knee in 2008, then in 2009, I had a partial knee replacement. I had a deposition in February 2011. They offered $5,000. The second time to New Jersey was in October 2011. They offered $15,000. I said no, saying I was a country pumpkin, then I went to court in Paterson, New Jersey. I felt like my attorney was trying to sell me out, so he gave up on the case. The judge in Paterson gave me twenty working days to find another attorney. I only lived five hundred miles away. I told the judge I was having a lot of pain driving up and back to North Carolina. He didn't. The third time to New Jersey was December 2011, almost four years since the accident happened. The court told me to wait by the phone if they needed me. Now I knew they were playing games with me. I was in much more pain now. I came home. My wife helped me out of the car.

On Christmas Day 2011 both knees buckled. I went to the doctor. I needed two total knee replacements. I wanted to die.

This is all about me loving my mother. I sent a medical letter and faxed it to cover me. The doctor said no more trips to New Jersey. On January 30, 2012, the court in Paterson and my attorney said I didn't notify the court or appear, so they dismissed the case that day.

On February 16, 2012, I had the first knee replacement. I tried many times to kill myself; it was affecting me mentally now. Thank God my wife kept copies of the faxes. They were all lying, and I proved it. The judge took it personally and made me pay for a deposition of $4,825 and three more trips to New Jersey. I went to court on December 2013. I started to cry on the stand. The judge let in another doctor's report for the insurance company. Guess who lost? I lost all my savings and maxed out my credit cards two times. My wife became my nurse. I was going on seven years with no paychecks, and I had to sell my home to pay medical bills. All for the love of my mother, I didn't pick up a drink, but this was the hardest thing I ever went through, drinking or sober. If I weren't sober almost eight years at the time of the accident, I don't know what I would have done dealing with life on life's terms. It can be hard at times—losing everything while sober.

I still pray to my Higher Power, Jesus, and ask AA for help to get through it. I'm sober, going on fourteen years now. My best day drunk isn't better than my worst day sober. I lost about $350,000 through this.

God bless you all.

Jersey Bill

About my book, *Alcoholism Taken Advantage of Drinking and Sober*, fourth story.

About Lawsuits

People don't understand that when you have a lawsuit, judges, insurance companies, and law firms are making deals already. Sometimes the deal doesn't help the person but helps the insurance company screw the person who got hurt. The law firm is offered a bigger case for more money. This will screw you. The judge must agree to this so everybody makes out but you. This is what's going on today in this country.

I still have a question: "How much does the judge make with these deals?" Well, I want the public to know this information.

God bless you all.

Jersey Bill

My book, *Alcoholism   Taken Advantage of Drinking and Sober*, fifth story.

About Car Insurance

I had one of these car insurance companies with their commercials on how they take care of disabled veterans. What a lie. I had damage done to my cars. When I bought my home, they gave me comprehensive coverage and took it away. I had an '88 Lincoln and a '77 El Camino. They gave me coverage on both, then when the damage was done to the '77 El Camino, they said it was too old; they couldn't cover it. So I took this insurance company to court. I won $1,350 in 2005. It's 2014, and they still haven't paid the judgment. The lady on that commercial is a liar. So don't let this happen to you. Make sure your insurance company doesn't screw you.

God bless you.

Jersey Bill

My book, *Alcoholism Taken Advantage of Drinking and Sober*, sixth story.

I Decided to Buy a New Truck

I went to a dealership here in Henderson, North Carolina. Talk about getting screwed with your pants on. I was sober for over ten years. I never owned a new truck. The dealer offered me this big deal. I should have known he was lying. I should have brought Vaseline with me; it would have gone in easier. Well, I decided on a 2008 truck. By the time I left, they screwed me out of two trucks, a 2003 and a '98 with a custom paint job. Then the 2008 was too big. I asked to bring it back. They gave me a 2010 in January 2011 at full value, $32,000, and I lost my two trucks for nothing. I'm a disabled veteran 100 percent. If they did this to me, I would watch out for grandmas and grandpas. Plus being a recovering alcoholic, I feel this is wrong.

I returned the truck in ten days. See, being sober, you have to learn to trust people, but dealerships don't care. Screw the customer, that's it. I got in touch with this car maker. They said they were not responsible for the dealerships. I told them, "They represent you." They didn't care.

I had driven their cars for years, but no more. I'll buy another car maker's car now.

God bless you all.

Jersey Bill

My book, *Alcoholism Taken Advantage of Drinking and Sober*, last story.

My Father's Friend

Today my father's close friend is still living. He's ninety years old. My father would have been eighty-three years old if he was still living. He talks about my father all the time. He told me, "Your father was one of a kind. If you were his friend, he would do anything in his power to help you." He said, "He loved to fight. He should have been a contender in boxing, and he was also the greatest street fighter I had ever seen. If you pissed him off, he would knock you out. That was one of his nicknames, Knockout or Little Jersey.

"One day your father and I were drinking beer outside a bar, and this black man was drunk, singing. This rookie cop told him he was causing problems. He said, 'Stop, or I will hit you with my nightstick.'

"Your father said, 'He's bothering nobody. Leave him alone.'

"The cop said, 'I'll hit you.'

"Your father knocked the cop out.

"One day we were in another city. Your father wanted another drink. The bartender started to jump at him. Your father knocked him out. Then he walked behind the bar and poured himself a drink. He was arrested and put in the jail cell. He started to bend the bars, destroying the jail cell. That how strong your father was. I never met a person that could do that. The police let him go."

This was the life my father lived. If you crossed him, he would hurt you. I know he put men in the hospital just with his hands. He still lives in his friends' hearts and my heart. He wasn't shown love, so he lived the way he did, but he always loved his family and friends.

God bless you all.

Jersey Bill